THIS BOOK BELONGS TO

_____

_____

*In Praise of*

# GRANDMOTHERS

FOUR SEASONS
PUBLISHING LIMITED

A grandmother should have wisdom beyond her years, and the patience of a saint. But above all she should have a very comfortable lap.

*Elizabeth Vardy*

To Angela, her grandmother was old but had not grown older and was never younger. This is a usual way with grandmothers.

*Cynthia Propper Seton*

I owe a debt to my grandmother for so much in my life. But what I owe her for most is my mother.

*Jane Achilles*

THE PUPPET SHOW
*Joseph Clark* 1834–1926

Little works of art displayed on cupboard doors,
   little works of art tucked in tiny drawers.
Grandma has a gallery that anyone can see,
   funny faces and small stick men.
And all were made by me.

*W. Morris*

Grandmas keep every drawing their grandchildren give them.
   They recognise their value. To her they are priceless.

*Violet Patience*

Grandma made my mother
the woman she is, and she made me.
So history repeats itself.

*Bethan Mai-Ling*

THE ARTIST'S
WIFE Katherine
*Frank Bramley*
1857–1915

MAKING SOUP
*C.V.M. Desleins*

*G*randmothers are usually
blessed with wisdom, beauty,
love and generosity in equal
proportions... and are totally
unaware of it.

*William Kennedy Scott*

*G*randmothers can do no wrong in
the eyes of their grandchildren.

*George Arthur*

*G*randmother — the creator of
a dynasty.
Teacher of the wise.
Physician to the infirm.
Counsel to the young.

*Kathleen Jones*

Grandma always just happened to be baking cakes when we visited and there always just happened to be enough cake-mix left in the bowl to scrape out with a wooden spoon. Grandmas always have perfect timing to make things just happen.

*Graham Keit*

Demi, as the oldest grandchild, then presented the queen of the day with various gifts, so numerous that they were transported to the festive scene in a wheelbarrow. Funny presents some of them, but what would have been defects to other eyes were ornaments to grandma's, – for the children's gifts were all their own.

*Louisa M. Alcott*

MAKING APPLE PIE
*Anonymous*

What is a grandmother?
Someone who is always available
for baby sitting,
knows everything, says nothing,
endures chocolate kisses and is
the proudest woman on earth.
That and her one hundred other duties.

*Elizabeth Vardy*

Just about the time a woman
thinks her work is done,
she becomes a grandmother.

*Margaret Fox*

FAMILY SCENE
*Eugenio Zampighi 1859–1944*

THREADING THE NEEDLES
*George Smith 1829–1901*

If becoming a grandmother was only a matter of choice, I should advise every one of you straight away to become one. There is no fun for old people like it.

*Hannah Whitall-Smith*

ON THE BALCONY
*Henry Schafer fl1870–1900*

Grandmothers are the bed-rock of the family,
they lay a solid foundation and add layer
upon layer of wisdom.

*Raymond George*

*T*he reason that
grandparents and
grandchildren get along so
well is that they have a
common enemy.

*Sam Levenson*

*T*he closest friends I have made
all through life have been people
who also grew up close to a loved
and loving grandmother
or grandfather.

*Margaret Mead*

A FRIEND IN NEED
*Robert Gemmell Hutchison* 1855–1936

DYED EGGS
*Robert Gemmell Hutchison* 1855–1936

Grandma was a kind of first-aid station or a red cross nurse who took up where the battle ended, accepting us and our little sobbing sins, gathering the whole of us into her lap, restoring us to health and confidence by her amazing faith in life and in a mortal's strength to meet it.

*Lillian Smith*

When a woman becomes a grandmother she suddenly doesn't mind admitting that she's over forty.

*D. R. Clayton*

If nothing is going well call your grandmother.

*Italian proverb*

To forget one's ancestors is to be a brook without a source, a tree without a root.

*Chinese proverb*

GRANDMOTHER'S BIRTHDAY CAKE
*Fritz Sunderland* 1836–1896

Whoever said that being a
grandmother gives all the enjoyment
of motherhood without any of
the work was obviously never
a grandmother!

*Erica Graves*

Perfect love sometimes does not come
until the first grandchild.

*Welsh proverb*

Years know more than books.

*Proverb*

THE CENTRE OF ATTRACTION
*James Hayllar 1829–1920*

Grandmother has a hymn-book with great silver clasps,
and she often reads in that book; in the middle of the book lies a
rose, quite flat and dry; it's not as pretty as the roses she has
standing in the glass; and yet she smiles at it most pleasantly of all,
and tears even come into her eyes. I wonder why grandmother
looks at the withered flower in the old book that way?

*Hans Christian Andersen*

The love between every grandmother and every grandchild is
a paradox – something in it is the same and something in it is
unique in every case.

*James Henry Lambert*

If there weren't any grandmothers –
where would we be?

*M. L. Van Hoecke*

THE CHRISTMAS TREE AT THE
DISPENSARY
*Henry Geoffroy* 1859–1944

*I*n the years since I began
following the ways of my
grandmothers, I have come to
value the teaching, stories and daily
examples of living which they
shared with me. I pity the younger
girls of the future who will miss
out on meeting some of these fine
old women.

*Beverley Hungry Wolf*

Y*our grandmother is someone who
manages to understand some of the
things your mother doesn't seem
quite to understand.

*Caroline Utley*

*T*here is no substitute for long
experience when giving sound advice.

*Japanese proverb*

≈

A grandmother is the one you go to
for a second opinion.

*Emily Wakefield*

≈

Little Peggy Simpson was standing at the door catching the
hailstones in her hand. She grows very like her mother. When she
is sixteen years old I dare say that to her grandmother's eye she
will seem as like to what her mother was as any rose in her
garden is like the rose that grew there years before.

*Dorothy Wordsworth*

≈

THE NEW DRESS
*John Callcott Horsley 1817–1903*

A grandmother always has time for you
when the rest of the world is busy.

*Georgina Sanders*

ALSO IN THIS SERIES

*In Praise of Children*
*In Praise of Daughters*
*In Praise of Friends*
*In Praise of Happiness*
*In Praise of Life*
*In Praise of Mothers*
*In Praise of Love*

Published by

FOUR SEASONS
PUBLISHING LIMITED

London, England

Text research by *Pauline Barrett*
Designed in association with *The Bridgewater Book Company*
Edited by *David Notley*
Picture research by *Vanessa Fletcher*
Printed in Dubai

Copyright © 1997 Four Seasons Publishing Ltd

All rights reserved.

ISBN 1-85645-513-0

ACKNOWLEDGEMENTS

Four Seasons Publishing Ltd would like to thank all those
who kindly gave permission to reproduce the words and visual
material in this book; copyright holders have been identified
where possible and we apologise for any inadvertent omissions.

We would particularly like to thank the following
for the use of pictures: *Bridgeman Art Library, e.t. archive,
Fine Art Photographic Library.*

Front Cover: THE SPINNING WHEEL, *Giovanni Battista Torriglia*, b. 1858
Title Page: GRANDMOTHER'S LESSON, *Silvestro Lega* 1826–1895
Endpaper: A FRIEND IN NEED, *Robert Gemmell Hutchison*, 1855–1936
Frontispiece: GRANDMOTHER'S BIRTHDAY, *Josef Laurens Dyckmans* 1811–1888
Back Cover: HERE'S GRANNY, *George Smith*, 1829–1901